GENDER-BASED VIOLENCE AND WOMEN'S RIGHTS

WOMEN
IN THE
WORLD™

GENDER-BASED VIOLENCE AND WOMEN'S RIGHTS

ZOE LOWERY AND LINDA BICKERSTAFF

Rosen
YA™

Published in 2018 by The Rosen Publishing Group, Inc.
29 East 21st Street, New York, NY 10010

First Edition

Library of Congress Cataloging-in-Publication Data

Names: Lowery, Zoe, author. | Bickerstaff, Linda, author.
Title: Gender-based violence and women's rights / Zoe Lowery and Linda Bickerstaff.
Description: New York : Rosen Publishing, [2018] | Series: Women in the world | Au-
dience: Grades 7–12. | Includes bibliographical references and index.
Identifiers: LCCN 2017010121 | ISBN 9781508174479 (library bound : alk. paper)
Subjects: LCSH: Women—Violence against—Juvenile literature. | Wife abuse—Juvenile
literature. | Sex discrimination against women—Juvenile literature. | Women's rights—
Juvenile literature.
Classification: LCC HV6250.4.W65 L69 2018 | DDC 362.88082—dc23
LC record available at https://lccn.loc.gov/2017010121

Manufactured in China

CONTENTS

On the night of January 18, 2015, two Stanford University graduate students were riding their bicycles home when they saw a man on top of a motionless woman. They were behind a dumpster; the woman was unconscious and some of her clothes were ripped off. The two students prevented the attacker, Brock Turner, from running away and held him until the police arrived.

In a widely publicized court case, the victim was repeatedly forced to relive her horrific experience. Brock Turner, a Stanford star swimmer, was eventually "convicted of sexual assault with an attempt to rape an intoxicated woman and sexually penetrating an intoxicated and unconscious person with a foreign object," reported the *Guardian*'s Sam Levin. He was sentenced to six months in county jail, but this sentence was curiously lighter than the state's recommendation of two years in the state prison.

Women have been subjected to violence since prehistoric times. Books such as the Bible and the Qur'an (Koran) have not only documented but condoned it; customs and laws have justified it. Violence against women is deep-seated in the conviction that, in short, women are less valuable than men.

In America, the colonists developed the laws with which they were familiar back in England. So colonial American women had only a few scant additional freedoms than slaves, servants, and children. Even without any kind of evidence, women and girls were accused of witchcraft and other practices, for which they were sentenced to death by men who made and enforced the laws. Wife beating, or chastisement, was a husband's legal right in the United States until the early 1870s. And it wasn't for another century that the law began to recognize violence against women. Fortunately, and finally, people who felt that women were experiencing discrimination in the United States united to start the feminist movement, which led the fight to end violence against women that persists today. It continues to affect women in every demographic and population all over the world, and includes the lesbian, gay, bisexual, transgender, and queer (LGBTQ) as well.

There is a small glimmer of hope amid the horrors experienced by Turner's victim's experience. The legislature of California passed a bill that would block judges from giving such light sentences in rape cases. According to a *Rolling Stone* article by Elias Leight, "'Sexually assaulting an unconscious or intoxicated victim is a terrible crime and our laws need

Bridget Bishop was just one of many women who suffered under scant colonial freedoms in America and was unjustly hanged when she was accused of witchcraft.

to reflect that,' Democratic Assemblyman Bill Dodd, who co-authored the bill, said in a statement. 'This bill is about more than sentencing,' he added. 'It's about supporting victims and changing the culture on our college campuses to help prevent future crimes.'"

Brock Turner has served his sentence. He served three months out of six, because of good behavior, and three years of probation. And the victim? She addressed Turner in court: "Your damage was concrete; stripped of titles, degrees, enrollment. My damage was internal, unseen, I carry it with me. You took away my worth, my privacy, my energy, my time, my safety, my intimacy, my confidence, my own voice, until today." Unfortunately, this victim's deep, quiet damage is too common.

CHAPTER 1

DOMESTIC AND INTIMATE PARTNER VIOLENCE

Domestic violence is the most common type of violence directed toward girls and women. The actual incidence of domestic violence in the United States is hard to determine because it is underreported. The Centers for Disease Control and Prevention (CDC) reports that as many as one in three women and girls experience physical abuse from a partner at some time in their life. As with nearly all types of violence against women and girls, men are usually— but not always—the perpetrators. A CDC survey found that "44 percent of lesbians and 61 percent of bisexual women experience rape, physical violence, or stalking by an intimate partner, compared to 35 percent of heterosexual women."

Every girl and woman in the world is at risk of being a victim of violence. Thalif Deen, the UN bureau chief for the Inter Press Service (IPS), in "Rights: UN Takes Lead on Ending Gender Violence," reports that UN Secretary-General Ban Ki-moon claims that one out of every three females in the world will be beaten, will be forced into having sex, or will otherwise be abused in her lifetime. Based on projected census data for 2010, Ki-moon's estimates mean that 52.7 million girls and women in the United States and 1.2 billion worldwide may eventually be victims of violence if something isn't done to stop it.

With some exceptions, the perpetrators of violence against girls and women are men. Jackson Katz, in his book *The Macho Paradox*, says that 90 percent of acts of violence against women occur at the hands of men. Ninety-nine percent of rapists are men. Who are these men? They are fathers, brothers, uncles, teachers, the guys next door, or any man. But a National Violence Against Women survey revealed that domestic violence is a very real part of life within the LGBTQ community as well: 35.4 percent of women living with a same-sex partner experienced domestic violence. And transgender individuals are not much better off, with 34.6 percent.

Sometimes domestic violence starts in small ways, such as jealousy over time and attention to friends, and escalates from there into more abusive behaviors.

DISTINGUISHING DOMESTIC VIOLENCE

The inception of domestic violence is often very subtle, such as a partner expressing jealousy when his or her girlfriend spends time with her friends. Or a spouse might disparage his or her dinner after the wife spent her entire day working on in the kitchen. Usually, the forcefulness increases a little more with each incident with a combination of several abusive behaviors. The Office on Violence Against Women lists them as:

- Physical abuse
- Sexual abuse
- Emotional abuse
- Economic abuse
- Psychological abuse

DEFINING DOMESTIC VIOLENCE

Violence against women is a crime punishable by law and a major public health issue. It is also a violation of the human rights of many women and girls in the United States and throughout the world. But what constitutes violence against women? A widely used definition of violence against women was given in resolution 48/104 passed by the United Nations (UN) General Assembly in 1993. *The Declaration of the Elimination of Violence Against Women* says that violence against women is any act, or even the threat of an act, against a girl or woman that results in

(Continued on the next page)

(Continued from the previous page)

physical, sexual, or emotional harm. The definition applies whether the act occurs in the privacy of a home or in a school, church, office, or other public place. This definition is the one that is used throughout this resource's discussion of violence against girls and women in the United States.

Domestic violence is also known as intimate partner violence, and is defined by the US Justice Department's Office on Violence Against Women as a pattern of abusive behavior, in any relationship, that is used by one partner to gain power and control over the other partner. The word "intimate" is often used to imply a sexual relationship between two people. In this case, the word has a broader meaning. It means a relationship between familiar people, including but not limited to family members, spouses, partners, children, or even caregivers.

PHYSICAL ABUSE

The use of physical force against someone in a manner that harms or endangers that person, known as physical abuse, is often a component of domestic violence. Hitting, shoving, biting, slapping, beating, cutting, shooting, or being forced to drink alcohol or take drugs are some examples of physical abuse.

Sometimes, physical abuse is so extreme that a girl or woman will require emergency medical attention for her injuries or she may die from them. Experts at the Family Violence Prevention Fund say that, on average, three girls or women are murdered by their boyfriends or husbands each day in the United States.

SEXUAL ABUSE

Sexual abuse is frequently a factor in domestic violence. It can range from verbal abuse of a sexual nature to unwanted touching to rape.

EMOTIONAL ABUSE

Emotional abuse occurs in all domestic violence situations. A victim of domestic violence who is told each day how worthless she is may lose her sense of self-respect. Her partner often convinces her that the entire situation is her fault. She may be so ashamed that she will cut herself off from friends and family members. Emotional damage can last a lifetime—long after physical injuries are healed.

ECONOMIC ABUSE

Economic, or financial, abuse occurs when the abusive partner maintains complete control over the couple's finances. The woman is given a small amount of money for household expenses and must account for every penny of it. Economic abuse can also involve stealing

A SUBTLE VIOLENCE: RELATIONAL AGGRESSION

The word "violence" usually calls to mind some type of physical act in which a person is injured. Acts that lead to emotional injuries can also be devastating. Their effects may be as long lasting as those caused by physical violence. A particularly hurtful type of emotional violence is relational aggression (RA). Researchers N. R. Crick and J. K. Grotpeter define RA as "behavior intended to harm someone by damaging or manipulating his or her relationship with others." RA happens more often among girls and is being seen at younger and younger ages. Examples of relational aggression include the following:

- Spreading rumors about another person.
- Making fun of another person.
- Calling another person by a nasty name.
- Excluding another person from a group or an activity.
- Revealing secrets that have been entrusted to you by another person.
- Making mean jokes about another person.

A girl who is a victim of RA is more likely to become a victim of other kinds of violence as a teen and later as an adult. Two programs that are dedicated to raising public awareness about RA as a type of violence against girls and women are the Ophelia Project and the Empower Program.

if the abuser actually removes money from joint bank accounts or sells mutually owned property without the consent of the victim of the abuse. This happens all too often in domestic violence involving older women who cannot care for themselves. Another manifestation of economic abuse occurs if women and girls are kept from furthering their educations or getting jobs that would allow them to be financially independent. Economic abuse is a major factor for women who want to escape abusive relationships. They often have no money or any way to earn money to support themselves outside of the relationship.

PSYCHOLOGICAL ABUSE

Much like emotional abuse, psychological abuse occurs in almost every domestic violence situation. The most frequent type of psychological abuse is intimidation. The abuser uses threats of physical violence against his partner, his children, or other family members

Intimidation is a common form of psychological abuse, which occurs when the abuser maintains control through threats of physical violence against his or her partner, children, or relatives.

to maintain control. He may also destroy property that his partner values. An especially cruel type of psychological abuse is the injuring or killing of a pet that is much loved by the victim. An abuser may also inflict psychological abuse by locking his victim in the house and not letting her out unless he is present. In J. D. Glass's article for *The Advocate*, Beth Leventhal, executive director of The Network/La Red in Boston, explained, "Abuse is not about violence; it's about control. You can be just as controlling of someone if you are small—as if you're large. It's about using violence or any other means of gaining and maintaining control."

A VICIOUS CYCLE

Domestic violence often occurs in dysfunctional relationships in which partners cannot or will not communicate. It may also occur if men have not learned appropriate ways to handle stress and anger. The so-called cycle of abuse, often discussed as a characteristic of domestic violence, is a manifestation of this inappropriate response to stress and anger. Here is how this cycle of abuse often works. It begins with the abuser getting angry and striking out at the victim with either words or actions or both. After this explosion of anger, the abuser appears to be ashamed, begs for forgiveness, and promises it will never happen again. He may even claim that he does not remember getting angry and acting violently. A peaceful period, often called a honeymoon period, follows. The victim of the violence begins to hope that all is well in the relationship. The abuser then gets angry again and the entire cycle is repeated. A woman may view her partner's "amnesia" about the anger and violence as a manifestation of illness in her abuser. Because she believes that her abusive partner is ill, she may choose to stay in the relationship.

Many abused women think that the notion of the cycle of abuse is nonsense. Abuse is always present at some level or another. For instance, during the so-called honeymoon period, the good times are still overshadowed by the dread and fear of impending violence and the stress of not knowing when it will erupt again. To these victims, the stress of never knowing for sure when they will be abused is worse than the abuse itself.

Many abused women also argue that intimate partner violence is systematic and intentional and not just something that happens spontaneously. For example, if a man gets angry with his partner in a grocery store or other public place, he waits until they are in private to abuse her. According to the LAWC, research also shows that men who physically abuse women inflict blows on areas of the body that are usually covered by clothes. This behavior strongly suggests that men are in total control of their anger, not out of control. They plan every episode of violence.

What domestic violence is really about is power and control. The LAWC describes a model of domestic violence proposed by Ellen Pense, founder of the Domestic Abuse Intervention Project in Duluth, Minnesota. This model, which is based on what Pense calls "a power and control wheel," describes the tactics that abusers use to exercise control over their intimate partners. Abusers shift or change tactics depending

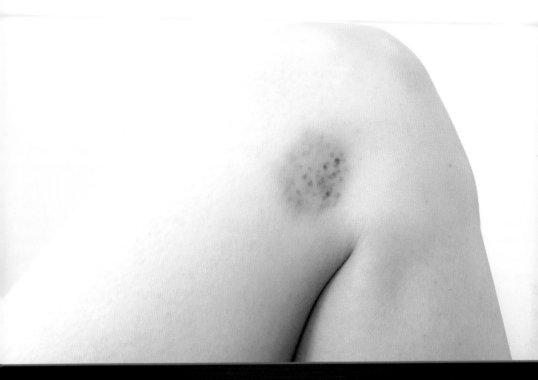

Many abusers are very intentional in their blows, choosing to hit their victim in areas they know will be covered by clothing and thus remain unseen to most people.

on what mood they are in, what the situation of the abuse is, and how their victims respond to the abuse. The model also suggests that abusers employ these tactics not only to control their partners but also to establish a relationship they can rely on in the future. In other words, abusers use various tactics to "train" their partners to give the responses they desire. Once the victim is trained, the abuser uses the same tactics over and over to reinforce the lesson.

MAKING IT PUBLIC

Until the early 1970s, domestic violence was not widely recognized in the United States. It wasn't until members of the feminist movement, and battered women themselves, began to develop shelters for abused women that the issue was brought to the attention of the American public. Even today, only about half of domestic violence incidents are reported to the police. Victims of domestic violence give many reasons for not reporting their situations. Brittney Nichols, a clinical psychologist and a victims' advocate at the East Texas Crisis Center in Tyler, Texas, took a survey of domestic violence victims with whom she worked. The survey showed that almost half of the victims did not report the incidents of violence because they believed nothing could or would be done about them.

Some women were afraid to report the violence because they were in the country illegally or their abusers held their documents of legal residence. To control them, abusers told the women that they would be deported if they reported being abused. However, deportation cannot happen in these cases. Law enforcement officers do not request residency status documents when they respond to domestic violence complaints. Immigration law requires that a woman be protected from domestic violence regardless of her residency status. Almost all the women who answered

If they are in the country illegally, some women are too frightened to report abuse out of fear that they could be deported. Sometimes, abusers reinforce this idea.

the survey were afraid that their intimate partners would become even more dangerous if they reported the abuse.

The Feminist Majority Foundation, an organization that works for women's equality, reproductive health, and nonviolence, says that women may be justified in failing to report domestic violence to the police. Many police departments do not have clear-cut procedures for handling domestic violence cases and fail to adequately document the extent of violence with photographs or other technical means. Even if arrested for assault, few men are prosecuted or convicted. Those who are convicted hardly spend any time in jail.

Lieutenant Richard Davis, a retired Brockton, Massachusetts, police officer and author, reports that mandatory arrest laws exist in twenty-four states. The remaining twenty-six states have preferred or pro-arrest laws that are similar to mandatory arrest laws. These laws require police officers to arrest all perpetrators of domestic violence regardless of what the act of violence is. A man who shoves his wife is as much at risk for being arrested as a man who viciously beats his wife.

Many people dealing with victims of domestic violence applauded passage of these laws. They felt that victims of domestic violence were being ignored when they reported that they were being abused. If ignored, the victims were at risk for severe injury or even death in subsequent acts of domestic violence. Davis believes that these laws are based on the false idea that most law enforcement officers do not care about domestic violence victims. He also points out that "one-size-fits-all" laws almost never accomplish what they were intended for because of the variability among situations in which they are applied. He strongly suggests that mandatory arrest laws be reexamined to see if they are effective. If not, he believes they should be abolished.

An unexpected result of these laws has been an increase in the number of women arrested for domestic violence. When officers arrive at the scene of a domestic violence incident, they may decide that both partners are acting aggressively and arrest them both. They don't take into account who is primarily responsible for the violence and who is acting in self-defense. Fortunately, many states are now developing policies and guidelines to help officers determine who the primary aggressor is in a violent incident. A primary aggressor is the person determined to be the most significant aggressor, rather than the first person to act aggressively. In most cases, the man is the primary aggressor and the woman is defending herself, and, all too often, her children. These guidelines may decrease the number of women being unjustifiably arrested in these situations.

GETTING OUT AND GETTING HELP

On the website TheLastStraw.wordpress.com, Rebecca J. Burns, a domestic violence survivor, says, "When I am asked why a woman doesn't leave [an] abuser, I say women stay because the fear of leaving is greater than the fear of staying. They will leave when the fear of staying is greater than the fear of leaving. At least this was true for me."

Every abuse situation is unique, but in every case leaving an abuser can be dangerous. Because most men and boys use the tactics of domestic violence to maintain power and control over their intimate partners, they consider separation or breaking up as a loss of power. It is important that both girls and women seek help as soon as they decide to leave an abusive relationship. *Maclean's* magazine author Celia Milne reports on a study by Helen Fisher, a professor of anthropology at Rutgers University in New Jersey. Fisher has shown in her study that men are most dangerous shortly after the breakup of a relationship. They have lost control and have been rejected by the person whom they most want to control. It is in the immediate days and weeks after a breakup that most domestic murders occur. A few steps to take to improve the odds of safely escaping from domestic abuse include the following:

- Girls should talk to their mothers or other responsible adults who can help them seek protection. They should choose safe places to have these conversations and should not use cell phones or text messaging to do so. Abusive boyfriends can monitor phones and computers.
- Girls or women who feel they are in immediate danger should call 911 and report the situation to the police.

- If injured, a girl or woman should go to a local hospital emergency room for treatment and protection.
- If a girl or woman is unsure of what to do, she should call the National Domestic Violence Hotline. Volunteers are available to provide the phone numbers of local domestic violence shelters and other resources.
- The number-one priority for both girls and women is to go somewhere that is safe. A safe house or women's shelter would be best. Not only are shelters safe, but also they are good places to get information about legal aid, counseling, and other services. Some shelters also provide the means to evaluate and monitor the abusive partner.

VISUAL, VERBAL, AND PHYSICAL: SEXUAL VIOLENCE

According to the Centers for Disease Control and Prevention, "Sexual violence is defined as a sexual act committed against someone without that person's freely given consent." But this is only a basic definition. The Rape, Abuse, and Incest National Network (RAINN) goes on to say, "The term 'sexual violence' is an all-encompassing, non-legal term that refers to crimes like sexual assault, rape, and sexual abuse...Please note that the legal definition of crimes vary from state to state. There are often other crimes and forms of violence that arise jointly with crimes like sexual assault."

TYPES OF SEXUAL VIOLENCE

There are many types of sexual violence, but they can be placed in three broad categories: visual sexual violence, verbal sexual violence, and physical sexual violence. Both visual and verbal sexual violence often precede physical sexual violence. A good example of

A stalker intends to scare the victim when he or she pur-

verbal and visual sexual abuse preceding physical abuse occurs in stalking. Stalking involves intentional and repeated episodes of following, watching, calling, e-mailing, texting, and other types of harassment that are intended to create fear in the person who is being stalked. Stalking is an extreme form of psychological abuse. Experts say that psychological abuse almost always precedes physical abuse. Many victims of physical sexual assault are stalked before being attacked.

VISUAL VIOLENCE

Visual sexual violence includes voyeurism and exhibitionism. Voyeurism is a type of sexual violence where a man gets sexual gratification from watching a woman in some intimate activity when she believes she is alone. For instance, a voyeur, who in slang terms is called a "peeping Tom," may stand outside an incompletely covered window and watch a woman undress or take a bath. Watching pornographic movies or looking at magazines or websites that show explicit sexual acts are also forms of voyeurism.

Exhibitionism is another form of visual sexual violence. This occurs when a man purposefully exposes his genitals in a public place. The man gets sexual gratification from the reactions of women who don't expect to see private parts in public places.

THE FIGHT AGAINST DIGITAL DATING VIOLENCE

In January 2009, three Pennsylvania high school girls were charged with disseminating child pornography after they sent nude photographs of themselves, which they had taken with their cell phones, to their boyfriends. The boys were charged with possessing child pornography after receiving the pictures on their phones. Stephanie Clifford, a correspondent for the *New York Times*, wrote that this behavior is not unusual in today's teen cyber world. As many as 22 percent of teen girls have been reported to have done the same thing, according to DoSomething. org. (Only about 18 percent of boys the same age have done so.) This is just one of the many activities that teens do that are classified in the Family Violence Prevention Fund's category of digital dating violence. Others include sending nonstop text messages or posting cruel comments on social media pages such as Facebook.

Alarmed by teens' use of digital technology to perpetrate violence, the Ad Council, a leading producer of public service advertisements that address the most pressing issues of the day, launched a public service ad campaign and established a website called

ThatsNotCool.com in February 2009 in partnership with the Family Violence Prevention Fund. Both the campaign and the information available through the website encourage preadolescents and teens to talk online with trained volunteers to learn about digital violence and what they can do to stop it. The goal is to help teens set their own boundaries and learn to tell their friends if they cross the line into "textual violence."

VERBAL VIOLENCE

Verbal sexual violence occurs when a man verbally threatens to sexually abuse a woman. Obscene phone calls are examples of verbal sexual abuse. In this cyber age, e-mail and text messages of a sexually explicit nature can also be considered verbal sexual abuse. This type of violence is extremely common. Abusers find it easier to violate their victims from afar than if the victims are there in person. Verbal sexual violence also occurs when teens, often on a dare, randomly call a girl with whom they are not acquainted and "do a little trash talk." It also occurs when rappers or singers use sexually explicit language in their songs, or actors in movies and on television speak about violent sexual acts.

33

PHYSICAL VIOLENCE

Physical sexual violence also takes many forms, including unwanted touching and sexual assault. Unwanted touching is sometimes called groping. The word "grope" means "to search out by feeling" but is frequently used in American slang to mean unwanted touching, fondling, or pinching of female breasts or genital areas. Groping occurs at unexpected times and in unexpected places. It often happens in crowded spaces such as in subways or elevators, or in the crush at sporting events or rock concerts. Regardless of where it happens, it is demeaning and a form of sexual violence.

Sexual assault is the ultimate form of sexual violence. Sexual assault includes rape, attempted rape, and other violent crimes that fall short of rape. The legal definition of rape is illegal bodily knowledge of a woman without her consent.

A VICTIM'S VULNERABILITY FACTORS

It is believed that most victims of sexual assault are girls and women. Boys and men can also be victims of sexual assault, but most of these cases are unreported. In a National Institute of Justice research report, Patricia Tzaden and Nancy Thoennes discuss what they call "vulnerability factors" for victimization. Several of the factors that make girls and women vulnerable to sexual assault include being:

- **Female.** It is thought that the majority of all rape victims are female.
- **Young.** According to the Centers for Disease Control and Prevention (CDC), about 42 percent of female victims were raped when they were younger than age eighteen; almost 30 percent were between the ages of eleven and seventeen; and about 12 percent were younger than age ten.
- **More trusting.** Very often, the abuser is someone trusted by the victim.
- **Poor.** Poverty makes girls and women vulnerable to sexual assault by making it difficult for them to support themselves financially. They may be forced to depend on abusive men for financial support. They may also be forced to engage in high-risk survival activities such as trading sex for food, money, or other items. They are also likely to live in slums, where violence is more common than in better neighborhoods.
- **Native American.** Almost a third of all rape victims in the United States in 2010 were Native American women, including Alaskan Native women, according to the CDC. The incidence

of rape or attempted rape of girls and women in other ethnic groups is lower: about 22 percent of non-Hispanic blacks, almost 19 percent of non-Hispanic whites, almost 15 percent of Hispanics, and about 35 percent of women of multiple races.

- **The victim of previous sexual violence.** Women who were assaulted as girls are two times more likely to be assaulted as adults than are women who were not victims of sexual assault in childhood.
- **Sexually promiscuous** (undiscriminating or loose). Women and girls who have many sexual partners, especially those who practice unsafe sex, are very vulnerable to sexual abuse.
- **Drunk or drugged-out.** Both alcohol and drugs make girls and women more vulnerable to sexual assault. The use of drugs and alcohol inhibits a person's judgment and frequently results in highly risky behavior.

Miriam Kaufman, an author and pediatrician working at the Hospital for Sick Children in Toronto, Canada, adds having disabilities to these vulnerability factors. Writing for the Committee on Adolescence of the American Academy of *Pediatrics*, Kaufman reports that children and teens with disabilities are twice as likely to be sexually assaulted as those who aren't disabled. The most vulnerable are young girls and teens

Studies show that teens with disabilities are more vulnerable, and thus doubly apt to be sexually assaulted and abused compared to those who are not.

with milder cognitive disabilities. Cognition involves thinking, reasoning, and problem solving. People with cognitive disabilities may be unable to do any of these skills well. These girls are very easy to abuse because they are especially trusting and obedient.

THE CONSEQUENCES: CHANGE

Change is the consequence of rape. The life of a victim of rape is changed from the minute she is raped. The CDC reports that rape and other types of sexual assault can cause long-term health problems, including chronic pain, headaches, stomach trouble, and psychological and emotional problems. Women who have been raped are often fearful and anxious. They may never trust any man again. This can lead to a woman's being unable to form a meaningful relationship with a man and to marital problems.

Adolescent girls react to being raped somewhat differently from the way adult women react to being raped. In her *Pediatrics* article, Kaufman wrote that girls who have been raped are more likely than their peers who have not been raped to:

- Have consensual (voluntary) sexual intercourse at a younger age.
- Practice unsafe sex, which may lead to pregnancy and the development of sexually transmitted diseases (STDs).
- Develop significant depression to the point of considering or attempting suicide.
- Develop self-harm behaviors, such as self-mutilation and eating disorders.
- Use alcohol and drugs.

Both girls and women may develop what is called rape trauma syndrome. In the initial phase of this syndrome, which usually lasts from days to

During the initial phase of rape trauma syndrome, the victim experiences a range of emotions that occur days or weeks after the incident.

weeks, victims experience disbelief, anxiety, and fear. They are on an emotional roller-coaster ride—angry one minute and sad the next. All of this is mixed with unjustified feelings of guilt as they wonder if they were somehow responsible for the rape. The second phase of the syndrome is the outward adjustment phase in which a girl generally resumes her everyday activities. She still has not come to terms with the rape and may be significantly depressed. The reorganization phase is the third phase of the syndrome. This may last from months to years. During this phase, victims go through periods of adjustment and eventually reach some level of recovery. The level of recovery achieved is different for every victim of rape. Some authorities consider rape trauma syndrome to be a form of post-traumatic stress disorder (PTSD).

THE CONSEQUENCES: STDS AND PREGNANCY

Rape victims can develop sexually transmitted diseases (STDs) following rape, but many girls and women who are raped are already infected. A study published in the *New England Journal of Medicine* reports that as many as 45 percent of rape victims had STDs at the time that they were raped. This number would be lower if girls were considered alone because only about 50 percent of girls have had sexual intercourse before being raped.

Getting the human immunodeficiency virus (HIV) is the main concern of most rape victims, although they are much more likely to get other types of STDs. The risk of getting HIV depends on how common it is in the community where the rape occurs and the nature of the rape. The likelihood that girls or women in the United States will get HIV after a single episode of rape is minimal. The likelihood of rape victims in African countries getting HIV, however, is

UNDER THE AGE OF CONSENT

Statutory rape is sexual intercourse with a person who is considered to be a minor. Attorney Jonna Spilbor says, "The idea behind statutory rape laws is that–in the eyes of the law–a person is incapable of consenting to various intimate acts until he or she reaches a certain age…States choose different, arbitrary numbers to approximate the age when they believe minors are mature enough to be able to meaningfully consent to sex." The age of consent in the various states ranges from twelve (in Oregon) to nineteen. Most states consider eighteen-year-olds to be capable of making adult decisions.

An article from the Community Crisis Center in Elgin, Illinois, reports that adult men father the majority of babies born to teenage mothers. Although as many as 20 percent of teen pregnancies result from forcible rape, many more result from statutory rape when a girl younger than the age of consent has consensual sexual intercourse with an adult male. By enforcing existing statutory rape laws and toughening others, authorities believe that most men will learn that girls are off limits. It is hoped that if men learn this lesson, the number of girls who find themselves pregnant and must deal with the problems that arise from being teen mothers will plummet.

much higher. Many men in Africa are HIV-positive or have acquired immunodeficiency syndrome (AIDS). Certain drugs, if given to a rape victim within twenty-four hours after the rape, will minimize the risk of contracting HIV by as much as 80 percent. There are few rape crisis centers in Africa to distribute drugs to help prevent abused women from getting HIV, and there is little money to pay for them. Girls who are victims of rape in the United States do have access to these drugs, however. If a girl or woman is raped by a man with AIDS, one who is known to be HIV-positive, or one who injects drugs, she should consider taking a course of the medications. Emergency room and rape crisis center personnel, as well as a personal physician, can help victims make decisions about treatment options if they are at high risk for getting HIV.

Pregnancy is also a possible consequence of

Pregnancy is a possible outcome of an unprotected sexual assault. The true numbers are difficult to know, but the US Department of Justice has suggested that between 7,750 and 12,500 children are conceived from rape each year.

rape. According to BBC author David Spiegelhalter, a European study showed that in general the chances of pregnancy after unprotected intercourse are about 1 in 20. RAINN reports that, based on statistics, in 2015, "On average, there are 288,820 victims (age 12 or older) of rape and sexual assault each year in the United States." The actual number is not known. RAINN also cites the US Department of Justice statistics suggesting, "children conceived from rape each year in the United States might range from 7,750–12,500." Again, the actual number is not known.

Regardless of what the number of pregnancies resulting from rape really is, it could be reduced if all rape victims were adequately cared for in health care facilities. Just as there are drugs that can lessen the risk of contracting HIV after rape, there are also medications that can almost completely eliminate the risk of pregnancy after rape. If taken within seventy-two hours (three days) of unprotected intercourse, emergency contraceptive pills, sometimes called "morning after pills," are up to to 89 percent effective in preventing conception and pregnancy, according to Planned Parenthood. Women, and especially teen girls, need to be educated about these drugs so that they will seek medical attention to obtain them if they are raped. This may help them avoid the potential risk of an unwanted pregnancy.

FALSE ACCUSATIONS OF RAPE

Just as rape itself is a devastating crime, falsely reporting a rape can be devastating for the man accused. In 2014, the venerable *Rolling Stone* magazine published a story that would cause ripples across the country, but not at all in the way it expected. Instead of bringing much-needed attention to the issue of sexual assault on college campuses, "A Rape on Campus: A Brutal Assault and Struggle for Justice at UVA" proved to be based on false accusations. Initially, the alleged victim, Jackie, claimed to have been raped repeatedly, or gang raped, by seven University of Virginia would-be fraternity members. Although the article's seasoned journalist, Sabrina Rubin Erdely, claims that at the time of publication she believed all the information to be accurate, further investigation by outsiders, including the *Washington Post*, revealed Jackie's claims to be untrue. The magazine published a retraction, but the damage was done, not only to reputations of the men involved, but also to the university.

The statistics surrounding false rape accusations have been as wildly deflated as they have been inflated. Some contend that the number is as low as 2 percent, arguing that rape is so devastating and shame-provoking that most girls and women do not want anyone to know that they have been raped. Reports by others, including some law enforcement personnel and prosecutors, say that as many as 40 percent of accusations of rape are false. In all likelihood, both of these numbers are out of line—one much to low and the other much too high.

The National Sexual Violence Resource Center puts the possible range of false accusations of 2 percent to 10 percent, based upon:

- "A multi-site study of eight U.S. communities including 2,059 cases of sexual assault found a 7.1 percent rate of false reports….
- A study of 136 sexual assault cases in Boston from 1998–2007 found a 5.9 percent rate of false reports….
- Using qualitative and quantitative analysis, researchers studied 812 reports of sexual assault from 2000-2003 and found a 2.1 percent rate of false reports."

When asked why a woman would falsely accuse a man of rape, Joseph Carver, a clinical psychologist, gave the following reasons:

- **To get revenge.** False accusation is an extreme way to punish someone.
- **To break up a relationship.** A daughter might accuse her stepfather of raping her to break up his marriage with her mother.

- **To gain legal advantage.** False accusation of rape or sexual abuse is often used in court to gain legal advantage in child custody cases during divorce actions.
- **To get attention.** This is an extreme attention-seeking strategy seen in individuals with personality or mental health problems.
- **To deflect responsibility.** A pregnant teenager might accuse a man of rape, rather than admit to her parents that she's sexually active.

The Innocence Project is a national public policy organization founded by two prominent attorneys. The goal of the project is to use scientific technology, including deoxyribonucleic acid (DNA) testing, to exonerate people who have been wrongfully imprisoned for crimes they did not commit. To date, 347 men have been released from prison, some of whom were wrongfully convicted of rape. Karen Stephenson summed up the issue in her article "False Allegations" by saying, "When men are falsely accused of rape, they become a victim of rape."

A DEFINITION IN QUESTION

The presidential race of 2016 turned out to be a surprising platform for the discussion of what constitutes sexual assault when candidate Donald

Trump was caught on video saying he could "do anything" he wanted to women, which, he went on to elaborate, included grabbing them by the genitals. Nevertheless, when he went on to be elected president, he announced that he planned to nominate Senator Jeff Sessions to the position of US Attorney General. Sessions defended Trump's actions, saying, "I don't characterize that as sexual assault," according to an article by Danielle Paquette in the *Washington Post*. Sessions later claimed his comments were misrepresented, leaving it alarmingly unclear how the potential US Attorney General defined sexual assault.

MYTHS AND FACTS

MYTH: Domestic violence is usually a onetime, isolated occurrence.

FACT: Domestic violence is characterized by repeated episodes of abuse.

MYTH: Girls and women entice men to rape.

FACT: Rape is the responsibility of the rapist alone. It is not the fault of the victim. Most rapes are planned. The rapist only waits for an appropriate opportunity and place to execute his plan.

MYTH: Few date rapes are "enabled" by the use of alcohol and drugs.

FACT: Alcohol and drug use before date rape is reported by more than 40 percent of teen victims of date rape and the same number of teen rapists.

CHAPTER 3

DANGEROUS DATING

A date should be lots of fun, but unfortunately this is not always the case. Date violence, according to the CDC, "is defined as the physical, sexual, psychological, or emotional violence within a dating relationship, including stalking. It can occur in person or electronically and might occur between a current or former dating partner. Several different words are used to describe teen dating violence:

- Relationship abuse
- Intimate partner violence
- Relationship violence
- Dating abuse
- Domestic abuse
- Domestic violence"

It is the most common type of violence against teen girls.

The notion of abusive teen relationships is relatively new, but violence among dating teens is as common as it is in adult marriages. A nationwide survey by the CDC "found that 23% of females and 14% of males who ever experienced rape, physical violence, or stalking by an intimate partner, first experienced some form of partner violence between 11 and 17 years of age." It is often difficult to recognize the early signs of date violence, but it is important to do so because they may be preludes to physical violence. Be wary of a dating partner if he or she does one or more of the following things:

- Makes fun of her or intentionally humiliates her in front of friends.
- Says she is worthless and without merit.
- Blames her for his or her bad feelings and mistakes.
- Criticizes all of her decisions and views.
- Belittles or makes light of her hopes, dreams, and achievements.
- Text messages or phones her many times throughout the day and night.
- Constantly tries to convince her to have sex and uses guilt to do so.

Physical violence among dating couples is the same as that inflicted in domestic violence. It includes restraining, pinching, kicking, choking, pushing, shoving, slapping, biting, burning, hair pulling, and

Physical violence is the same whether you're dating or married. Abusive partners may kick, pinch, choke, bite, or force sexual activity (among other actions) on their partner.

sexual assault, among other actions. Sexual assault in the setting of date violence is any type of sexual activity that is forced on a girl by her dating partner. It includes rape and attempted rape.

DATE OR ACQUAINTANCE RAPE

Date rape, also called acquaintance rape, is rape that occurs between two people who are dating or who know each other. In "What EVERY Guy Must Know

About Date Rape," Mike Hardcastle, a special needs foster parent, youth adviser, and author, says, "Call it date rape, call it acquaintance rape, or just call it what it is, rape; whatever you call it, it's a crime and it is committed at a shocking rate of every two minutes in North America." Yes, date rape is rape, but it is different from rape by a stranger in several ways.

Perhaps the most significant of these differences is that girls are more vulnerable to date rape than to rape by a stranger. It is hard for a girl to believe that a guy she really likes and has admired can be a rapist. Scott Linquist, a rape prevention specialist, reports that 84 percent of all rapes are date or acquaintance rapes. In his book *The Date Rape Prevention Book*, Linquist says that girls and women are especially vulnerable to rape by men they know. They are taught to be wary of strangers, but they let down their guard with dates, friends, and acquaintances.

When a girl is raped by a stranger, she is often beaten and otherwise injured as well as being raped. In date rape, such violence is less common, although it can occur. Even though a girl has no bruises or other physical injuries, if she is penetrated in any way, she has been raped. Rape victims, especially date rape victims, may find that they can never trust men again. Far beyond the physical trauma of rape, the loss of trust may be the most significant consequence of rape.

STAY SAFE AND PREVENT RAPE!

Henry de Bracton, a British judge, noted in his 1240 book, *On the Laws and Customs of England*, "An ounce of prevention is worth a pound of cure." That says it all when it comes to rape. It is far better to prevent rape than to have to deal with the consequences. Here are a few recommendations from the American Academy of Pediatrics to help girls avoid being raped:

- Don't attend parties given by unknown people.
- Don't meet with people known only from Internet contacts.
- Don't walk alone at night.
- Don't pose for nude or sexually explicit photographs.
- Don't use drugs of any kind.
- Don't drink from anything that has been left unattended.
- Don't accept drinks from a stranger.
- Do go to parties with a "buddy," and stay in touch with that friend.

DRUGS AND ALCOHOL

Alcohol and drugs are major factors in date rape. Linquist calls them "rape enablers." In spite of recent media coverage about date rape drugs, alcohol is still the major enabler of date rape. Most people think that alcohol is a stimulant because they initially feel better when they use it. The "lift" that people feel with its use is really a loss of inhibitions, not stimulation. Alcohol is actually a depressant. In large enough quantities, it causes people to get sleepy. It also decreases male sexual performance. That is why most men with date rape in mind tend to minimize their own alcohol consumption.

They furnish their dates with lots of alcohol while drinking little themselves. Sooner or later, a girl will fail to say no or may become incapable of saying no. At that point, sexual intercourse becomes rape.

Drugs such as marijuana and cocaine have been enablers of date rape for years. There are three drugs, however, that are specifically known as date rape drugs. These are Rohypnol (the brand name for flunitrazepam),

The idea that alcohol stimulates date rape aggressors is not necessarily true. They are more likely to use it to get their victims too drunk to refuse.

GHB, and ketamine. The street names for Rohypnol include roofies, ruffies, roche, R2, Mexican Valium, rib, forget-me-pill, and rope, among other names. It is a medication that is usually prescribed as a sleeping pill in Europe and Latin America. It's illegal in the United States. Besides causing drowsiness and a loss of inhibitions and judgment, it can also cause amnesia. The original Rohypnol was a white tablet that dissolved quickly in liquids. It added no taste, color, or odor to beverages. The manufacturer of Rohypnol has since changed the appearance of the pill. The tablet is olive-green, with a center of blue specks. In pale-colored beverages, it turns the drink blue to show the drink has been drugged. (Generic versions do not have this dye, though.)

GHB is gamma hydroxybutyrate. Its nicknames include grievous bodily harm, liquid ecstasy, cherry meth, goop, and scoop. GHB was originally developed as an anesthetic to put people to sleep before surgical procedures. It causes unconsciousness and amnesia, qualities that make it a perfect date rape drug. Unfortunately, it can also cause some life-threatening symptoms, such as reduced heart rate, seizures, and respiratory failure. It is particularly dangerous when used with alcohol. GHB comes in a liquid form, so it can easily be added to a date's drink.

Ketamine is also called special K, super K, cat valium, k-hole, purple; it was originally produced for use as an anesthetic for people and by veterinarians

Because GHB (gamma hydroxybutyrate) is a liquid, it is easily added to a date's beverage, causing her to become unconscious, but it can be life-threatening when mixed with alcohol.

working with large animals. It can be obtained legally by prescription for those purposes. Among its side effects are confusion, lack of coordination, and amnesia in those recovering from its use. Ketamine is also extremely dangerous when used with alcohol.

HELP AT YOUR FINGERTIPS?

Undercover Colors, founded by four male engineering students from North Carolina State University, is "wearable nail tech that identifies the presence of common date rape drugs in a variety of beverages through color change." The website goes on to explain: "The only perfect solution to drug induced sexual assault is ending it altogether. As we all work toward that ideal, Undercover Colors' technology provides wearable protection at your fingertips. Simply dip your finger into a verified beverage and within seconds the presence of prevalent date rape drugs will be identified in color change."

The product has yet to hit the shelves, and already it has some criticisms, such as the fact that alcohol itself is most commonly used to drug a date. Furthermore, if women are among people they already know, they are less guarded and less likely to think that they even need to check their drink. Still, the nail polish could prove to be a useful tool.

DATE RAPE DRUG VICTIM?

Because victims of date rape in which date rape drugs were used may not remember the incident, they may need to look for clues to determine if it really happened. An article on date rape drugs on TeenAdvice.about. com suggests looking for the following clues. A date rape victim may:

- Feel "hung-over" despite having ingested little or no alcohol.

- Have a sense of having had a hallucination or a very "real" dream.
- Have fleeting memories of feeling or acting intoxicated, although she did not use alcohol.
- Have no clear memory of events during an eight-to-twenty-four-hour period.
- Be told stories by others about how intoxicated she seemed at a time when she knew she had not used alcohol or drugs.
- Experience pain and discomfort in her vagina.

A girl who strongly suspects that she was drugged and then date raped should go to a health care facility or to her personal physician as soon as possible. Blood tests may confirm the presence of remaining date rape drugs in her system if her blood is drawn within twelve-to-twenty-four hours of the drug being ingested.

Feeling hung over (though you weren't drinking), vivid dreams or hallucinations, and trouble remembering the past day are some clues that you may have consumed a date rape drug.

WHAT TO DO IF YOU ARE RAPED

Rape is a major trauma. It is experienced as a loss of control. Too often, it renders a girl or woman incapable of doing much of anything. That is one of the reasons why rape is an underreported crime. Authorities on rape say there are steps that a rape victim should and should not take.

- Get to a safe area as quickly as possible.
- Go to a hospital emergency room to get a medical exam in which specimens are collected that can help identify the rapist.
- Report the crime to police, school authorities, campus police, or emergency medical personnel.
- Call a trusted friend or family member for support during examinations.
- Contact a rape crisis center for understanding, support, and information.
- Get counseling.

Victims should *not* do any of the following because they may destroy evidence that is needed to identify and convict the rapist:

- Shower, bathe, douche, or otherwise clean up before going to an emergency room or rape crisis center.

Even if you think you're fine, rape is a major trauma. Reaching out to a rape crisis center or counselor can be an invaluable source of support.

- Change clothes before going to an emergency room or rape crisis center.
- Straighten up the house or apartment if it was the scene of the rape.

Many rape victims consider it a sign of weakness to ask for help after they have been raped. To the contrary, getting counseling is a healthy sign—one that says a victim wants to take back control of her life. She wants to be a survivor of rape, rather than a victim of it. To get the most help from counseling sessions, it is beneficial for a girl or woman to have questions in mind that she needs answered. (See the sample questions to ask a counselor.)

Don't expect to notice benefits from counseling right away. While some victims only need one or two sessions before they feel like they start to recover and accept what has happened to them, others simply need much more time. In either case, it is crucial to listen to the advice of a counselor and continue with sessions until he or she feels you are ready to stop. Seek out one of the many support groups, where one can get help from people who have also been victims of rape.

10 GREAT QUESTIONS TO ASK A COUNSELOR

1. Was the rape my fault?

2. Did the way I dressed or acted lead to my rape?

3. Will I be raped again?

4. How can I protect myself in the future?

5. Will I get HIV?

6. Will I get pregnant?

7. How can I learn to trust men again?

8. If I report the rape, what will happen to the rapist?

9. Are there any agencies that will help me pay for counseling?

10. How can I help prevent other girls from being raped?

CHAPTER 4

BY AND WITHIN THE MILITARY

Domestic violence subjects are often the top stories in newspapers, news websites, and television's prime-time news. Sexual assault is a particular issue within the US military, so much so that other United Nations countries, such as Denmark and Slovenia, have spoken out about the US military's inaction on the matter. Women do not serve in the military in every country, but where they do, such as in Israel, Canada, the United Kingdom, Eritrea, and Peru, studies (which have been scant up to this point) are beginning to show that military violence against women needs attention there, too.

BY THE US MILITARY

Conquering armies often believe that, as the victors, they are entitled to use and abuse the girls and women of the clans, tribes, or countries that lose the war. Unfortunately, some US troops believe the same thing. Despite the efforts of military leaders to prevent it, some US military personnel are still assaulting and raping local female residents in the countries where they are stationed. Recent examples of this include sexual assaults on some of the girls and women in Iraq.

Ruth Rosen, a journalist and professor of history and public policy at the University of California, Berkeley, wrote in "The Hidden War on Women in Iraq," "Iraqi women, like women everywhere, have always been vulnerable to rape." She reports that since the American invasion of Iraq, the problem has worsened. Women are literally disappearing from public life as they imprison themselves in their homes. It seems better to stay at home than to risk sexual assault by some American soldiers or kidnapping and abuse by uncontrolled local gangs. A specific example given by Rosen is the case of Abeer Qassim Hamza al-Jabani, a fourteen-year-old Iraqi girl who was raped and killed by five US soldiers. Her body was set on fire to cover up the crime, and her parents and sister were murdered. Since the incident, three of the soldiers have been tried and found guilty of rape and murder.

Some Iraqi women are practically imprisoned in their own homes, which feels like a better option than going out and risking rape or sexual assault.

Two will serve sentences of ninety years or more in military prison. The third was sentenced to twenty-seven months in prison, while a fourth has yet to be tried. The fifth man, who was the ringleader of the group, was discharged from the military before details of the rape and murders were known. He awaits trial in a civilian court. Many Iraqi citizens believe that none of these sentences were severe enough.

Incidents of sexual assault of female inmates at Abu Ghraib, a prison run by the US military in Iraq, have been videotaped. These videos have been reviewed by military leaders and members of the US Congress who are developing ways to crack down on violence against women by US military personnel. The videos reportedly show multiple episodes of rape perpetrated by some American soldiers on Iraqi female prisoners. These incidents are just a few of the abuses allegedly committed by some US troops in Iraq.

WITHIN THE US MILITARY

Women have been serving in the US military since the Revolutionary War. But it was not until President Harry S. Truman signed the Women's Armed Services Integration Act in 1948, however, that women finally gained professional military status. The Women's Armed Services Integration Act limited the number of women in the military to 2 percent of the total force and spelled out what military occupational specialties (MOS) women could fill.

At the present time, women fill almost every MOS, with the exception of combat slots. According to the *Military Times*, as of January 2015, women made up about 201,400 women on active duty in the US military: about 68,900 in the Army, 57, 300 in the Navy, 58,500 in the Air Force, and 14,100 in the Marines. Of around 71,400 soldiers deployed at that time, 9,200 were women. One of the arguments used against women serving in combat positions is that if they become prisoners of war, they are likely to be sexually abused by enemy forces.

Sadly, the greatest risk of sexual abuse for women in the military comes from their comrades-in-arms. In an article for Truthout by H. Patricia Hynes, Helen Benedict, a journalism professor at Columbia University in New York City who writes extensively on social justice and women, quotes one soldier: "The mortar rounds that came in daily did less damage to me that the men with whom I shared my food." And this is not just one case. This soldier's experience was echoed time and time again in Benedict's research.

In 2014, an independent survey reported by the *Military Times* cites that of 170,000 troops, "20,000 servicemembers said they had experienced at least one incident of unwanted sexual contact in the past year, representing nearly 5 percent of all active-duty women and 1 percent of active-duty men." A 2014 RAND National Defense Research Institute's independent survey looked at issues of sexual assault, sexual harassment, and gender discrimination within the military. It included 560,000 service members, and looked at assaults by other service members, civilians, spouses, or others. They found that 20,000 had been through one or more sexual assaults, whether they were rape, attempted rape, and sexual crimes that did not involve penetration. Of this sampling, 1 in 20 women were sexually assaulted, which works out to about 8,600 women. (It also reported that 1 in 100, or about 11,400 men, were sexually assaulted as well, showing that while this is a serious matter for women, men are far from immune from it.)

The *Military Times* reported a more sinister fact as well. Women (and men) reported that many acts were extremely violent: "just 29 percent of assaults against women and 11 percent against men in 2014 would have been classified as penetrative sexual assaults." The term "penetrative sexual assaults refers to crimes that "include rape and penetration with an object," according to the report.

In 2015, according to the Department of Defense, they "received a total of 6,083 reports of sexual assault for allegations involving service members. In addition, climate survey results indicate that over 16,000 service members intervened in situations they believed to be at risk for sexual assault."

REMEMBERING FOUR OF FORT BRAGG'S FALLEN

On October 8, 2008, a vigil was held at the gates of Fort Bragg, one of the US Army's largest military bases. The vigil was held to commemorate the lives of four US military women who had been murdered in North Carolina in the nine months preceding the vigil. An editorial published in the Fayetteville, North Carolina, *Observer* said, "It's an old argument, we train men, and now women, to wage war, then we are baffled when they do that to each other…In a way it's surprising that there aren't more bodies piling up at military bases all over this nation." Although preventive measures are being taken by the military to stop violence against its women, they are obviously not enough. One of the purposes of the vigil, which was kept by forty men and women, was to call for renewed efforts to prevent further deaths. In writing about the vigil for TruthOut.org, Ann Wright, a retired army colonel and former diplomat who resigned from the US State Department in protest over the Iraq War, said, "Sadly, no one from the Military Command Authority nor from the prevention of domestic violence offices at Fort Bragg made the effort to come to the gates to talk about ending the epidemic of violence."

THE MILITARY AND MISOGYNY

According to Benedict, military women are raped twice as often as their civilian counterparts. Benedict says sexual violence persists in the military because of a "confluence of military culture, the psychology of the assailants, and the nature of war." Military culture contributes misogyny, or the hatred of women, to the equation. She believes that misogyny "lies at the root of why soldiers rape." Men who enter the military, says Benedict, are made to feel that they won't fit in unless they harass and belittle women whenever they can. It's the macho thing to do, so even the "nicest guys" may find themselves assaulting women.

Several scholars whom Benedict mentions have investigated the psychology of assailants. These include criminologist Menachim Amir and psychologists

Women may have made great gains in their military careers, but they are raped two times as often as civilian women.

Nicholas Groth and Gene Abel. The conclusions that these men drew from their separate studies were similar. They found that rapists are not motivated by lust but by a mixture of anger, sexual viciousness, and the need to dominate someone. Benedict also refers to work by Rutgers University law professor Elizabeth Hillman that suggests today's all-volunteer army is attractive to men who are prone to rape because these men perceive that violence is acceptable in a military setting.

The nature of war also contributes to violence against women. Benedict says that Robert Lifton, distinguished professor of psychology and psychiatry at John Jay College in New York City, has studied and written extensively about war and war crimes. He believes that soldiers are particularly prone to commit atrocities in certain types of war. Wars that have no well-defined armies and have been justified by false information or lies are those in which many atrocities occur. It was difficult in the war in Vietnam, and it is equally challenging in the present wars in Iraq and Afghanistan for US military personnel to identify the enemy. Enemy armies are not well defined. Some soldiers have a very hard time justifying what they are ordered to do, so they come to loathe themselves. They may express their self-hatred, as well as their fear and anger, by acting violently against those around them. Too often, these are the military women with whom they serve.

TREATING MST

Several steps have been, and continue to be, taken to treat the victims of what is called military sexual trauma (MST) and to correct practices within the military that lead to it. Treatment of victims of MST usually falls to VA medical personnel because victims on active duty are hesitant to report the crime for fear of retaliation and harassment by their male colleagues. They wait

Army veteran Kate Weber spent seventeen years healing from military sexual trauma (MST). Today, she advocates for

until they leave the military, and then seek treatment. The aftereffects of sexual trauma, as reported by retired military women being cared for in VA medical facilities, include the following:

- They avoid places or objects that cause them to recall the traumatic incident.
- They frequently feel that something is missing or not right.
- They may abuse alcohol and drugs.
- They sometimes develop severe depression with suicidal thoughts.
- They have recurring and intrusive thoughts and dreams about the traumatic incident.
- They have many nonspecific health problems.
- They develop relationship problems.

Since 2002, the VA has screened all (male and female) discharged military personnel for MST. The VA is making structural changes in existing facilities and is opening new facilities to specifically treat women with MST. These centers provide inpatient and outpatient care and counseling to MST victims.

INTERVENE, ACT, MOTIVATE

Stopping the violence is as important as treating MST. Many efforts have been made to do so, but the apparent

Army Veteran Orlinda Marquez and her puppet Henry stand beside her artwork, which depicts stages of her MST recovery. Some MST survivors heal by expressing themselves through art.

increase in the number of cases reported would suggest that efforts have been inadequate. In March 2008, the US Department of Defense released its fourth annual report on sexual assault in the military. Amie Newman, managing editor for *RH Reality Check*, an online publication advancing sexual and reproductive health and rights, says that the report again showed an increase in the number of assaults on military women. She goes on to say that the US House of

Representatives Subcommittee on National Security and Foreign Affairs held a hearing on sexual assault in the military on July 31, 2008. Representative Louise Slaughter of New York reintroduced a bill called the Military Domestic and Sexual Violence Response Act that, had it passed, would have established an Office of Victims Advocate (OVA) within the Department of Defense. It would have strengthened policies for reporting, prosecuting, and treating perpetrators, and expanded counseling and treatment programs for victims through the VA. Unfortunately, although a new version of the bill was introduced in 2009, it was never enacted.

As part of its Sexual Assault Prevention and Response program, the US Army has instituted "I AM Strong" ("I AM" stands for "Intervene, Act, Motivate"), which calls for soldiers to confront peers who are abusing alcohol or participating in other behaviors that could lead to sexual assault. Soldiers are expected to alert higher-ranking personnel if their colleagues' behavior does not improve. Skeptics believe that this program is unlikely to work, as similar programs have failed in the past. Most critics believe that the military's effort to combat sexual violence has been hampered by a lack of support from some senior commanders. In 2017, the program was still going strong, at http://www.sexualassault.army.mil.

In 2013, New York's Senator Kirsten Gillibrand introduced the Military Justice Improvement Act (MJIA), which "is designed to reverse the systemic fear that survivors of military sexual assault describe in deciding whether to report the crimes committed against them." Although it was not readily passed. Gillibrand continues to support MJIA and speak out against military sexual assault.

CHAPTER 5

SEEKING SOLUTIONS

After a long history of acceptance of assault against women simply being the norm, it is finally considered, in both the United States and internationally, to be a top public health concern. According to the CDC, "The combined medical, mental health, and lost productivity costs of [intimate partner violence] against women are estimated to exceed $8.3 billion per year." Clearly, violence against women just has to be stopped.

ON THE FEDERAL LEVEL

Prior to 1990, there were many US Codes (laws), including the Victims of Crime Act of 1984 (VOCA), addressing violent acts in general. Congress passed the VOCA because of the explosion of violence in the United States during the 1970s and early 1980s. In 1990, additional legislation was introduced in Congress to supplement the VOCA. At the same time, Representative Pat Schroeder of Colorado and Senator Joe

Pat Schroeder, with then-Senator Joe Biden, introduced legislation that resulted in the Violence Against Women Act, a part of the Violent Crime Control and Law Enforcement Act

Biden of Delaware introduced legislation in the House and the Senate to specifically address issues of violence against women. Congress passed the Violence Against Women Act (VAWA) in August 1994, as part of the Violent Crime Control and Law Enforcement Act.

The VAWA was considered by most authorities to be a vital first step in America's efforts to recognize and treat violence against women as a serious problem. In explaining the provisions of the act, experts at the Family Violence Prevention Fund say that it made domestic violence and sexual assault crimes punishable by law. It also provided funding for several programs to encourage states to address domestic violence and sexual assault. Other grants were given to educate police, other law enforcement personnel, and prosecutors about violence against girls and women. Emphasis was placed on the need to treat victims as victims, not as perpetrators. Diana Russell, professor emeritus of sociology at Mills College in Oakland, California, and one the world's foremost experts on sexual violence against women, gives an example of this need in her book *The Politics of Rape*. A woman that she interviewed while writing her book said, "When a person is robbed, the robber is put on trial. When someone is murdered, the murderer is tried. But when a woman is raped, it is the woman and not the rapist who is put on trial."

The VAWA also established the Office of Violence Against Women within the US Department of Justice, and it authorized and funded a National Domestic Violence Hotline. Congress reauthorized the act in both 2000 and 2005. In 2013, President Barack Obama signed into law the Violence Against Women Reauthorization Act of 2013 (VAWA 2013), which officially took effect on March 7, 2015.

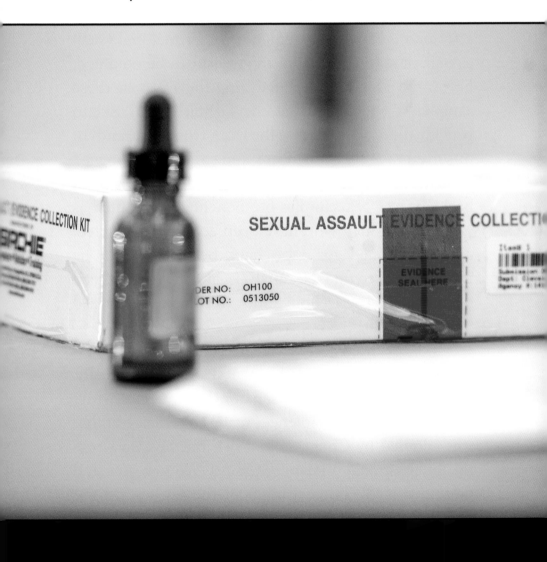

In 2004, Congress passed a second piece of legislation, the Debbie Smith Act. With advancement in the technology to analyze DNA, law enforcement officials and courts were given tools to solve rape cases that they had not previously had. DNA is the material in body cells that carry a person's genetic code (genome). No two people have exactly the same genetic code. If a woman is raped and semen or other material (such as hair or skin cells) from the rapist can be obtained, he can be identified by analyzing the DNA in these samples. Congress passed the Debbie Smith Act to provide funding to process the DNA from thousands of unsolved rape cases that were, and still are, backlogged in state and local crime laboratories. The processing of backlogged DNA samples has benefited some men as well. Several men who have been accused, convicted, and imprisoned for rape have been found to be innocent, based on DNA analysis, and have been freed from prison. The Debbie Smith Act was reauthorized in 2008 and 2014.

Joseph Biden, 47th vice president of the United States (2008–2016), has been a strong advocate for women's rights. As a US senator, he not only wrote and introduced the Violence Against Women Act that was adopted by Congress in 1994, but he also wrote the International Violence Against Women Act and presented it to Congress in 2007. The act is a historic and unprecedented effort by the United States to address violence against women globally. In 2014, he and then-President Barack Obama designed the White House Task Force to Protect Students from Sexual Assault. Additionally, the vice president co-chaired the White House Council on Women and Girls.

The Obama administration was also proactive in LGBTQ issues, with additional funding for community services that help LGBTQ people. Furthermore, the Office on Violence Against Women and the Family Violence Prevention and Services Program set out regulations about how to handle LGBTQ issues, with additional information on how to make services applicable to trans and queer people.

EDUCATORS STEP UP

Following several episodes of violence in which girls were injured or killed by former boyfriends while at school, educators are stepping up to try to stem the violence. In "Killings Prompt Efforts to Spot and Reduce Abuse of Teenagers in Dating," *New York Times* correspondent Elizabeth Olson reports on several programs underway. For example, Texas adopted a law that requires school districts to define dating violence in school safety codes. This was prompted by the stabbing death of Ortralla Mosley, a fifteen-year-old, in a hallway of an Austin, Texas, high school and the shooting death of Jennifer Ann Crecente, an eighteen-year-old.

THE FIGHT BY COMPANIES AND FOUNDATIONS

On November 26, 2008, the Robert Wood Johnson Foundation announced eleven recipients for funding in a new program called Start Strong: Building Healthy Teen Relationships. According to a spokesperson for the Family Violence Prevention Fund, which is a partner in the program with the Robert Wood Johnson Foundation, $18 million are being invested by the foundation over four years to help prevent teen dating violence and sexual abuse. Most recipients of the funding are schools or health care facilities, each of which will receive about $1 million to finance their programs. Each group will work with students in the sixth through eighth grades, using older teens as mentors. The programs will, among other things, train older teens, teachers, coaches, and parents in methods to promote healthier teen relationships.

Since 1991, the clothing company Liz Claiborne, Inc., has been working to end domestic violence through its Love Is Not Abuse program. The program provides information and tools that men, women, children, teens, and corporate executives can use to learn more about the issue of domestic violence and how they can help end this epidemic.

The Avon Foundation for Women also helps in the fight against domestic violence through its Speak Out Against Domestic Violence program. The Avon Foundation for Women has contributed more than $580 million to stop domestic violence throughout the world, including the NO MÁS Study ("No More", a study of Latin American domestic violence and sexual assault), Avon Regional Domestic Violence Grants Program, Campus Sexual Assault Prevention Programs, Global Partnership to End Violence Against Women, and Justice Institute on Gender-Based Violence.

Singer, songwriter, and actress Fergie is just one in a long line of high-profile celebrities to speak out for Avon's Speak Out Against Domestic Violence program.

Also mentioned in this article is the Lindsay Ann Burke Act that was passed by the Rhode Island legislature in 2007. This act requires all middle and high school students in Rhode Island to take educational programs to learn about the widespread dangers of dating violence. Lindsay Ann Burke was a twenty-three-year-old who was murdered by an abusive former boyfriend. Her mother, Ann Burke, teaches health classes in a Rhode Island middle school. She helped to push this act through the legislature and has developed programs to educate teachers about the subject. Although the programs will vary from school to school, all will be aimed at helping students appreciate the extent and dangers of dating violence.

TEENS TAKE ACTION

Violence against girls and women is an epidemic that is difficult to treat. Like almost any epidemic, it is far better to prevent it than to try to treat it. The most important step in preventing this epidemic is to educate young people and get them involved in helping to stop the violence. Several outstanding programs have been developed by and for teens. Only a few are presented here. Each of them has the same goal—to stop the violence.

Students Taking Action for Respect (STAR) began in 2001 because students in several Texas high schools realized how big a problem dating violence and sexual abuse had become. At that time, a survey showed that three out of four Texans between the ages of sixteen and twenty-four had experienced abuse in a dating relationship or knew someone who had. The STAR program, under the guidance of the Texas Association Against Sexual Assault (TAASA), provides youth with leadership skills and the knowledge to talk to their peers about the issues of dating violence and sexual abuse. There are now more than four hundred youth leaders throughout Texas who present programs on sexual and dating violence to their peers in schools and community groups. The program has reached more than 13,000 students in 130 communities so far.

Launched nationally in 2006, Choose Respect is a program developed by the Division of Violence Prevention of the CDC to help adolescents form healthy relationships to prevent dating abuse before it starts. The program is aimed at young people from eleven to fourteen years of age because they are still forming attitudes and beliefs that will affect how they are treated and how they treat others. Choose Respect publicizes its messages through e-cards, posters, bookmarks, pocket guides, online games, television and radio programs, and other media.

On a Friday night in 1989, Alex Orange died trying to break up a fight at a party. His friends didn't just send flowers to his funeral—they also formed Students Against Violence Everywhere (SAVE). In the twenty years since this student-driven organization was formed, it has expanded its membership to 200,000 teens in more than 1,700 SAVE chapters across the United States. The various programs sponsored by SAVE teach teens that there are alternatives to violence and provide opportunities for them to practice what they learn through school and service projects. Dating violence is covered in the programs of this group.

Break the Cycle states, "Everyone has a right to a safe and healthy relationship, regardless of gender, ethnicity, or sexual identity. We work every day to make that right a reality." Beginning in Los Angeles, California, in 1996, they provided "teen-specific violence prevention education and providing legal services for youth." Today, the program is active in Los Angeles and the District of Columbia, with partners, volunteers, and supporters all over the country.

Another bright spot in the fight to stop violence against women is the role that some men are taking to stop the violence. Coaching Boys into Men is an example of one of the programs developed by men for men and boys. This program invites men to be part of the solution for stopping violence against girls and women by teaching boys that violence never equals strength. The Family Violence Prevention Fund and the Waitt Institute for Violence Prevention are its cosponsors. The institute is funded by the Waitt Foundation, which was formed by Ted Waitt, founder of Gateway Computers. Before the program started,

BYRON HURT'S CALL TO MEN AND BOYS

Byron Hurt was a young boy when hip-hop appeared in the Bronx, one of the boroughs of New York City. He is now an internationally known filmmaker. He was also one of the founders of the Mentors in Violence Prevention (MVP) program, which is "the leading college-based rape and domestic violence prevention initiative for college and professional

(continued on the next page)

Byron Hurt poses at a screening of his documentary, *Hip-Hop: Beyond Beats & Rhymes*, which takes a look at hip-hop's portrayal of manhood, sexism, and homophobia.

(continued from the previous page)

athletics." He has also been an associate director of the US Marine Corps' first programs to help stop gender violence.

His hour-long documentary, *Hip-Hop: Beyond Beats & Rhymes*, made in conjunction with the Independent Television Service, examines how manhood, sexism, and homophobia (hatred of homosexuals) are presented in hip-hop culture. It looks at hip-hop through the eyes of a fan, specifically focusing on the tendency of some aspects of hip-hop to suggest that manhood or masculinity requires "real men" to bash girls, women, and gays. The film was a 2006 Sundance Film Festival Selection. It was produced for the PBS series *Independent Lens* and aired on February 20, 2007, to kick off the Hip-Hop National Community Engagement Campaign. The campaign was designed to educate kids who buy and listen to rap and watch music videos—and those who make them—about the potential harm of some of the messages being presented. The film and an extensive program developed around the message of the film are being used as teaching tools in many high schools and in various youth organizations throughout the country. Hurt says, "I made the film to let boys and men know that sexism is unacceptable and that men can and should condemn it."

Hurt continues to make films, write, and speak out about race, class, and gender.

surveys showed that fewer than 29 percent of men talked to boys about violence against girls and women. Since 2000, the number of men who actively talk to boys about violence has increased significantly. A spokesperson for the Family Violence Prevention Fund says, "True progress toward ending violence against

Some groups, like the Delaware Coalition Against Domestic Violence, use a purple ribbon to symbolize and raise awareness for domestic violence. October is Domestic Violence

women and children will only be achieved when a critical mass of men are actively involved in the solution by talking to the boys in their lives."

Violence against girls and women is a national and worldwide problem of epic proportions. Acts of domestic violence, dating violence, and especially violence toward women in the military are underreported. The problem of violence against girls and women is actually much worse than it appears. The causes of the violence are many and deeply rooted in cultures and traditions that imply that women are inferior to men and should therefore be controlled by them. Although laws are in place to punish men who act violently against women, these are not the solution to the problem. The only way to stop the violence is to teach children at an early age that it is wrong. Older teens, parents, teachers, coaches, religious leaders, and members of the media need to remember that they are setting the example that children and adolescents will follow. This is a grave responsibility for those who want to stop the violence.

Girls and women in the United States may be subjected to violence anywhere and at any time: at home, while out with friends, at work, or when they least expect it. Women in the US military are as likely to be harmed by their comrades as by the enemy. By looking at the similarities and the differences among the many types of violence against women, people can gain a better understanding of what the challenges are for stopping it. Efforts to fight violence against girls and women are being made at all levels of government, but the programs that are most effective are those initiated by and for teens. Your actions and words may ultimately prove to have the greatest effect in winning the war against violence against women.

AGGRESSOR A person who attacks or act hostilely toward another person.

AMNESIA Loss of memory.

ANTHROPOLOGY The scientific study of the origin and the physical, social, and cultural development and behavior of humans.

CHASTISEMENT Punishment, especially a beating.

CONDONE To overlook or excuse.

CONFLUENCE The process of coming together.

ENTICE To tempt, attract, or seduce.

FEMINIST A person, either a man or a woman, who supports legal, economic, and social equality between the sexes.

INCIDENCE The extent or frequency of the occurrence of something.

INITIATE To bring about a new measure or program.

MISOGYNY Being adverse to, feeling scorn for, or feeling bigotry against women.

PATRIARCHY A culture or society characterized by the supremacy of the father in the family.

PERPETRATOR The person responsible for an action.

PORNOGRAPHY Obscene, lewd, or immodest photographs, writing, or painting, usually of a sexual nature.

POST-TRAUMATIC STRESS DISORDER (PTSD) An anxiety disorder associated with serious traumatic events and characterized by symptoms of survivor guilt, nightmares, flashbacks, and depression.

PRELUDE An introductory action or event.

RESTRAIN To tie up or keep under control in some manner.

SPONTANEOUS Acting impulsively or without planning.

SYSTEMATIC Methodical in conduct or performance; well-thought-out; the opposite of spontaneous.

Break the Cycle
P.O. Box 811334
Los Angeles, CA 90081
(424) 265-7346
P.O. Box 66165
Washington, D.C. 20035
(202) 849-6289
Website: http://www.breakthecycle.org
Break the Cycle is a national nonprofit organization
    that engages, educates, and empowers youth to
    build lives and communities free from dating
    and domestic violence.

Canadian Women's Foundation
133 Richmond Street NW, Suite 504
Toronto, ON M5H 2L3
Canada
(416) 365-1444 or (866) 293-4483
Website: http://www.canadianwomen.org
Canadian Women's Foundation is Canada's
    only national public foundation dedicated to
    improving the lives of women and girls.

Men Can Stop Rape
1130 6th Street NW, Suite 100
Washington, DC 20001
(202) 265-6530
Website: http://www.mencanstoprape.org
Email: info@mencanstoprape.org
This group works to build young men's capacity
    to challenge harmful aspects of traditional
    masculinity in order to prevent men's violence
    against women.

National Aboriginal Circle Against Family Violence
Canadian Women's Health Network
419 Graham Avenue
Winnipeg, MB R3C 0M3
Canada
(613) 236-1844
E-mail: cwhn@cwhn.ca
Website: http://www.cwhn.ca/en/node/19898
This organization focuses on reducing family violence and hopes to someday eliminate it in Canada's Aboriginal communities.

National Coalition Against Domestic Violence
One Broadway, Suite B210
Denver, CO 80203
Phone: (303) 839-1852
Email: mainoffice@ncadv.org
Website: http://www.ncadv.org
This organization is dedicated to the empowerment of battered women and is committed to the elimination of personal and societal violence in the lives of battered women and their children.

National Domestic Violence Hotline
PO Box 161810
Austin, TX 78716
(800) 799-7233
Website: http://www.thehotline.org
This hotline was established in 1996 as a component of the VAMA and provides crisis intervention, information, and referrals to more than 5,000 shelters and domestic violence programs nationwide.

97

National Organization for Women
1100 H Street NW, 3rd Floor
Washington, DC 20005
(202) 628-8669
Website: http://www.now.org
This is the largest organization of feminist activists
    in the United States. Its goal is to bring about
    equality of women and eliminate discrimination,
    harassment, and violence against women.

National Teen Dating Abuse Helpline
P.O. Box 161810
Austin, TX 78716
(866) 331-9474
Website: http://www.loveisrespect.org
This helpline is operated by the National Domestic
    Violence Hotline and offers real-time, one-on-
    one support from trained peer advocates. They
    can be reached by text messaging by texting
    loveis to 22522.

The NW Network
P.O. Box 18436
Seattle, WA 98118
(206) 568-7777
Email: info@nwnetwork.org
The NW Network was founded in 1987 by lesbian
    survivors of abuse. The NW Network endeavors
    to cease abuse in LGBTQ communities through
    education, organizing, and advocacy.

Rape Abuse and Incest National Network (RAINN)
2000 L Street NW, Suite 406
Washington, DC 20003
(202) 544-1034
Website: http://www.rainn.org
RAINN provides information on resources throughout the country for survivors of rape, abuse, and incest. It maintains the National Sexual Assault Hotline, (800) 656-4673 (HOPE), and an online chat: online.rainn.org.

US Department of Justice Office on Violence Against Women
145 N Street, NE, Suite 10W.121
Washington, D.C. 20530
(202) 307-6026
Email: ovw.info@usdoj.gov
Website: http://www.usdoj.gov/ovw
This office is responsible for the overall coordination and focus of the DOJ's efforts to combat violence against women.

WEBSITES

Because of the changing nature of internet links, Rosen Publishing has developed an online list of websites related to the subject of this book. This site is updated regularly. Please use this link to access this list:

http://www.rosenlinks.com/WITW/violence

Burns, Kate, ed. *Violence Against Women.* Farmington Hills, MI: Greenhaven Press, 2008.

Dressen, Sarah. *Dreamland.* New York, NY: Speak/ Penguin Group, 2012.

Finn, Alex. *Breathing Underwater.* New York, NY: HarperCollins, 2012. Ebook.

Gerdes, Louise I. *Domestic Violence* (Opposing Viewpoints). New York, NY: Greenhaven Press, 2011.

Haley, John, Wendy Stein, and Heath Dingwell. *The Truth About Abuse.* New York, NY: Facts on File, 2010.

Kaplan, Arie. *Dating and Relationships: Navigating the Social Scene* (A Young Man's Guide to Contemporary Issues). New York, NY: Rosen Publishing, 2012.

Levy, Barrie. *In Love and in Danger: A Teen's Guide to Breaking Free of Abusive Relationships.* Paradise, CA: Seal Press, 2008.

Lily, Henrietta M. *Dating Violence* (Teen Mental Health). New York, NY: Rosen Publishing, 2012.

Mabry-Gordon, Sherri. *Are You Being Abused?* New York, NY: Enslow Publishing, 2016.

Picoult, Jodi. *The Tenth Circle*, 2nd ed. Sydney, Australia: Allen & Unwin, 2015.

Piehl, Norah. *Date Rape.* New York, NY: Greenhaven Publishing, 2013.

Piercy, Marge. "Rape Poem." *Circles on the Water, Unabridged*. New York, NY: Knopf, 2015.

Sherman, Michelle, and De Anne Sherman. *Finding My Way: A Teen's Guide to Living with a Parent Who Has Experienced Trauma*. Edina, MN: Beaver's Pond Press, 2009.

Wilkins, Jessica. *Date Rape* (Straight Talk About). New York, NY: Crabtree, 2011.

"About Vice President Biden's Efforts to End Violence Against Women." The White House. Retrieved November 26, 2016. https://www.whitehouse.gov/1is2many/about.

Avon Foundation. "Avon Foundation News." June 8, 2008. http://www.avoncompany.com/women/news/press20080608.html.

Benedict, Helen. "Why Soldiers Rape." 2008. http://www.inthesetimes.com/article/3848.

Burns, Rebecca. "Quotes About Domestic Violence." August 15, 2007. http://thelaststraw.wordpress.com/2007/08/15/quotes-about-domestic-violence.

Carver, Joseph. "Why Would a Woman Falsely Accuse Someone of Rape?" December 3, 2008. http://counsellingresource.com/ask-the-psychologist/2008/12/03/false-accusation-of-rape.

Centers for Disease Control and Prevention. 2016. http://www.cdc.gov.

Clifford, Stephanie. "Teaching Teenagers About Harassment." *New York Times*, January 26, 2009. http://www.nytimes.com/2009/01/27/business/media/27adco.htr.

Community Crisis Center. "Teen Pregnancy and Sexual Assault." 2004. http://www.crisiscenter.org/TeenPregnancy.html.

Davis, Richard. "Mandatory Arrest: A Flawed Policy Based on a False Premise." March 31, 2008. http.//www.policeone.com/writers/columnists /RichardDavis/articles/1679122-Mandatory -arrest-A-flawed-policy-based-on-a-false- premise.

Deen, Thalif. "Rights: UN Takes Lead on Ending Gender Violence." United Nations, February 26, 2008. http://ipsnews.net/news .asp?idnews=41356.

Department of Defense. "DoD Releases FY15 Annual Report on Sexual Assault in the Military." May 5, 2016. http://www.defense.gov/News/News -Releases/News-Release-View/Article/752270 /dod-releases-fy15-annual-report-on-sexual -assault-in-the-military.

DoSomething.org "11 Facts About Sexting." Retrieved November 21, 2016. https://www.dosomething .org/us/facts/11-facts-about-sexting.

Family Violence Prevention Fund. 2008. http://www .endabuse.org.

Feminist Majority Foundation. "Domestic Violence Facts." 2007. http://feminist.org/other/dv/dvfact .html.

Gillibrand, Kirsten. "Comprehensive Resource Center for the Military Justice Improvement Act." The Office of Kirsten Gillibrand, 2015. http:// www.gillibrand.senate.gov/mjia.

Hardcastle, Mike. "What EVERY Guy Must Know About Date Rape." Updated April 28, 2016. http://teenadvice.about.com/od/daterape/a/daterapeguysfyi.htm.

"H.R. 840 — 111th Congress: Military Domestic and Sexual Violence Response Act." www.GovTrack.us, 2009. https://www.govtrack.us/congress/bills/111/hr840.

Hurt, Byron. "Byron Hurt." Retrieved November 26, 2016. http://www.bhurt.com.

Hynes, H. Patricia. "Military Sexual Abuse: A Greater Menace than Combat." Truthout, January 26, 2012. http://www.truth-out.org/news/item/6299-military-sexual-abuse-a-greater-menace-than-combat.

Independent Television Service. "Hop-Hop: Beyond Beats & Rhymes." 2008. http://www.itvs.org/outreach/hiphop/gender.html.

Innocence Project. "Exonerate the Innocent." 2016. http://www.innocenceproject.org/exonerate.

Jenny, C., T. Hooton, A. Bowers, M. Copass, J. Drieger, S. Hillier, N. Kiviatt, L. Corey, W. Stamm, and K. Holmes. "Sexually Transmitted Diseases in Victims of Rape." *New England Journal of Medicine*, Vol. 322, No.11, March 15, 1990, pp. 462–470.

Katz, Jackson. *The Macho Paradox*. Napersville, IL: Sourcebooks, 2006.

Kaufman, Miriam. "Care of the Adolescent Sexual Assault Victim." *Pediatrics*, Vol. 122, August 2008, pp. 462–470.

Landau, Elaine. *Date Violence*. New York, NY: Franklin Watts, 2004.

Leight, Elias. "Brock Turner to Be Free After Three Months for 'Good Behavior.'" *Rolling Stone*, August 30, 2016. http://www.rollingstone.com /culture/news/brock-turner-to-be-released -from-jail-for-good-behavior-w436997.

Linquist, Scott. *The Date Rape Prevention Book*. Naperville, IL: Sourcebooks, 2000.

Military Times. "Incidents of Rape in Military Much Higher than Previously Reported." Retrieved November 23, 2016. http://www.militarytimes .com/story/military/pentagon/2014/12/04/iraq -immunity/19888635.

Milne, Celia. "Breakup Blast: Rejection Can Trigger a Brain 'Primed to Do Something Dangerous.'" July 25, 2006. http://www .macleans.ca/science/technology/article .jsp?content=20060731_131152_131152.

Newman, Amie. "Congress Hears Voices of Sexual Assault Survivors in Military." *RHRealityCheck*. org, July 31, 2008. http://www.rhrealitycheck.org /blog/2008/07/31/congress-hears-voices-sexual -assault-survivors-military.

Nichols, Brittney. "Violence Against Women in the U.S. Is a Serious Problem." *Violence Against Women*. Farmington Hills, MI: Greenhaven Press, 2008.

NIDA Blog Team. "What Are Date Rape Drugs and How Do You Avoid Them?" National Institute on Drug Abuse for Teens, March 16, 2015. https://teens.drugabuse.gov/blog/post/what-are-date-rape-drugs-and-how-do-you-avoid-them.

Office of Violence Against Women. "Fact Sheets." U.S. Department of Justice, 2007. http://www.ovw.usdoj.gov/ovw-fs.htm.

Ophelia Project. "Relational Aggression." http://www.opheliaproject.org/main/relational_aggression.htm.

Paquette, Danielle. "It's Not Clear If Jeff Sessions Thinks Grabbing a Woman by the Crotch Is Sexual Assault." *Washington Post*, November 18, 2016. https://www.washingtonpost.com/news/wonk/wp/2016/11/18/its-not-clear-if-trump-attorney-general-sessions-thinks-grabbing-a-woman-by-the-crotch-is-sexual-assault.

Planned Parenthood. "Morning-After Pill (Emergency Contraception)." 2016. https://www.plannedparenthood.org/learn/morning-after-pill-emergency-contraception.

Rape, Abuse, and Incest National Network. 2016. http://www.rainn.org.

Rosen, Ruth. The Hidden War on Women in Iraq. Women's International League for Peace and Freedom, July 13, 2006. http://www.peacewomen .org/news/Iraq/July06/The_hidden_war_on _women.html.

Russell, Diana. The Politics of Rape. Lincoln, NE: iUniverse, 2003.

Sampson, Ovelta. "Girls Talk! 'Relational Aggression' as Harmful as Any Schoolyard." Gazette (Colorado Springs), April 29, 2002. http://findarticles.com /p/articles/mi_qn4191/is_20020429/ai_n100c.

Shapiro, T. Rees. "'Our Worst Nightmare': New Legal Filings Detail Reporting of Rolling Stone's U-Va. Gang Rape Story." Washington Post, July 2, 2016. https://www.washingtonpost.com/news/grade -point/wp/2016/07/02/our-worst-nightmare -new-legal-filings-detail-reporting-of-rolling -stones-u-va-gang-rape-story/.

Spiegelhalter, David. "Sex: What Are the Chances?" BBC. March 15, 2012. http://www.bbc.com /future/story/20120313-sex-in-the-city-or -elsewhere.

Spilbor, Jonna. "Is the Recent Spate of High-Profile Teen Pregnancies, Including Bristol Palen's, Jamie Lynn Spears's Telling Us It's Time to Alter Statutory Rape Laws?" Find Law, September 16, 2008. http:// writ.lp.findlaw.com/commentary/20080916 _spilbor.html.

Stephenson, Karen. "False Allegations." May 14, 2007. http://abuse.suite101.com /article.cfm/false_allegations.

Students Against Violence Everywhere. "History." 2007. http://www.nationalsave.org/main/history .php.

Teen Advice. "Date Rape Drugs: Date Rape Drugs Explained a Demystified." http://teenadvice .about.com/library/weekly/aa062502a.htm.

Texas Association Against Sexual Assault. "Students Taking Action for Respect." 2008. http://www .taasa.org/star.

Undercover Colors. Retrieved November 23, 2016. http://www.undercovercolors.com.

United Nations. "Declaration on the Elimination of Violence Against Women." 1993. http://www .stopvaw.org/Declaration_on_the_Elimination _of_Violence_Against_Women3.

US Department of Defense. "Women's History Month." Retrieved November 23, 2016. http:// archive.defense.gov/home/features/2015/0315 _womens-history.

Wright, Ann. "Military Town Newspaper Challenges U.S. Military in Murder of Military Women." October 17, 2008. http://www.truthout .org/101708J.

ABOUT THE AUTHORS

Zoe Lowery is an avid student of history, with a particular interest in women's roles. When she's not writing or editing, Lowery enjoys experimenting with recipes in the kitchen or riding her motorcycle over the mountains or to her local library in Colorado.

Linda Bickerstaff is a retired general and peripheral vascular surgeon who has cared for victims of domestic violence, dating violence, and sexual assault in emergency rooms and operating rooms. She also has a dear friend whose life was threatened by an abusive husband. It has taken years for the friend to escape the nightmares of that experience. Bickerstaff has written several books for Rosen Publishing, including *Cocaine: Coke and the War on Drugs* (Drug Abuse and Society) and *Modern-Day Slavery* (In the News).

PHOTO CREDITS

Cover Jetta Productions/Blend Images/Getty Images; pp. 8–9, 79 Bettmann/Getty Images; p. 12 tommaso79/iStock/Thinkstock; p. 18 ViewApart/iStock/Thinkstock; p. 21 IpekMorel/iStock/Thinkstock; p. 23 Juanmonino/iStock/Thinkstock; pp. 26, 30, 59 KatarzynaBialasiewicz/iStock/Thinkstock; p. 34 omgimages/iStock/Thinkstock; p. 38 Manuel Faba Ortega/iStock/Thinkstock; p. 40 stock-eye/iStock/Thinkstock; p. 43 b-d-s/iStock/Thinkstock; p. 52 lolostock/iStock/Thinkstock; p. 55 diego_cervo/iStock/Thinkstock; p. 57 Stockphoto24/iStock/Thinkstock; p. 61 Wavebreakmedia/iStock/Thinkstock; p. 66 DEA/Archivio J. Lange/De Agostini/Getty Images; p. 68 James Whitmore/The LIFE Images Collection/Getty Images; p. 71 KaninRoman/iStock/Thinkstock; p. 73 The Washington Post/Getty Images; p. 75 Andy Cross/Denver Post/Getty Images; p. 81 Christian Science Monitor/Getty Images; p. 85 Dimitrios Kambouris/Getty Images; p. 89 Hal Horowitz/WireImage/Getty Images; p. 91 ThitareeSarmkasat/iStock/Thinkstock; cover and interior pages (globe) LuckyDesigner/Shutterstock.com; cover and interior pages background designs lulias/Shutterstock.com, Dawid Lech/Shutterstock.com, Transia Design/Shutterstock.com.